CONTENTS

CW00815975

COMMITMENTS

In our learning and meeting together we commit to...

- holding each other before God in prayer

- praying for the presence and guidance of the Holy Spirit in all our conversations

- learning together from Scripture and from each other

- listening well and enabling everyone to speak

- making space for those whose voices have not yet been heard to contribute – but without putting people on the spot if they don't wish to speak

- avoiding interrupting each other – instead, acknowledging what others say before moving on to have our say

- keeping confidential anything personal that is shared (unless it is a safeguarding matter)

- taking care about how we speak about others who are not in the room

- looking out for and being sensitive to people's feelings

- giving each other time to reflect before sharing with others

- taking time out as a group from time to time, offering one another an opportunity to say if there is anything in the discussion they have found difficult but haven't been able to express

- learning together how we can live more fully in the way of Christ.

INTRODUCTION

The fruit of the Spirit is
love, joy, peace, patience,
kindness, generosity, faithfulness,
gentleness, and self-control.
There is no law against such things.
(Galatians 5.22–23)

The purpose of this course is to help church communities to examine afresh their life and learning together in the face of difference and diversity. It is based on the Church of England's 'Pastoral Principles for Living Well Together' (**www.churchofengland.org/PAG**). Although the Pastoral Principles were developed to encourage better inclusion of LGBTI+ people, they can be applied to other differences within our church communities.

In this course we are invited to think about the things which impair relationships. The Pastoral Principles identify six 'pervading evils': prejudice, silence, ignorance, fear, hypocrisy and power. These 'evils' hinder our personal growth as Christians, hurt other people, and create barriers that stop our churches from growing into Christian communities of welcome and belonging. They are the opposite of the fruit of the Spirit. It is easy to see these 'evils' in others; the hard work is to see them within ourselves.

When there are strongly held differences among us, we are tempted to form like-minded groups or factions. Communities that become divided in this way is one of the greatest challenges for our Church and society today. We can all play a part in seeking unity in our Church as well as in the wider community. This course encourages us to find creative ways to grow and learn together in the love of Christ.

Each of the five sessions in this course is accompanied by a short film. These films are extracts from the Living in Love and Faith Course. They relate the Pastoral Principles to questions of identity, sexuality, relationships and marriage. However, this course can be used to explore any topic about which there are different views and experiences within a church community or group.

A PRAYER
to begin each session

Heavenly Father,
you have called us in the Body of your Son Jesus Christ
to continue his work of reconciliation
and reveal you to the world:
forgive us the sins which tear us apart;
give us the courage to overcome our fears
and to seek that unity which is your gift and your will;
through Jesus Christ your Son our Lord,
who is alive and reigns with you,
in the unity of the Holy Spirit,
one God, now and for ever.
Amen.

Common Worship: Collect for The Unity of the Church

SESSION ①

Listening and speaking – addressing **IGNORANCE** and paying attention to **POWER**

The AIMS of this session are

- To be more aware of our ignorance about each other's experiences, challenges and perspectives
- To learn to listen more attentively and to speak more bravely in order to get to know each other better
- To notice how power affects our relationships and church communities
- To be more careful about the way power is handled in our church communities

① Course film

Watch the Session 1 video.

② Bible study

Read the text out loud slowly. Allow some silence afterwards.

Philippians 2.1–11

If then there is any encouragement in Christ, any consolation from love, any sharing in the Spirit, any compassion and sympathy, [2] make my joy complete: be of the same mind, having the same love, being in full accord and of one mind. [3] Do nothing from selfish ambition or conceit, but in humility regard others as better than yourselves. [4] Let each of you look not to your own interests, but to the interests of others. [5] Let the same mind be in you that was in Christ Jesus,

[6] who, though he was in the form of God,
did not regard equality with God
as something to be exploited,
[7] but emptied himself,
taking the form of a slave,
being born in human likeness.
And being found in human form,
[8] he humbled himself
and became obedient to the point of death—
even death on a cross.
[9] Therefore God also highly exalted him
and gave him the name
that is above every name,
[10] so that at the name of Jesus
every knee should bend,
in heaven and on earth and under the earth,

¹¹ and every tongue should confess
   that Jesus Christ is Lord,
   to the glory of God the Father.

Here is an activity for you to do together as a group.

Invite the group to form pairs with a person they don't know very well.

Each person in the pair listens to the other speaking about what captured their imagination about the text and what question arose for them (3 minutes each person).

Call the group together and ask each person to share what their partner said.

Ask the group, 'What might God be up to in the passage for us today?'

③ Reflect and discuss together

Listening shows that we don't want to be **IGNORANT** of each other's experiences and perspectives. It has been said that we can't understand someone until we have walked a mile in their shoes. Philippians 2 reminds us that God knows what it is like to be human because in Jesus, God took our human form. He walked in our shoes.

Church communities are full of people with different backgrounds, experiences and views. As we gather around the Communion table, we are reminded that we are one body, bound together in the love of Christ. This is a wonderful reality, and quite remarkable. But how well do we know each other?

It is very easy to stereotype people and assume we know what they think. Really getting to know someone who is different to us requires time, openness and courage. It involves exploring each other's views and listening to each other's stories, as well as engaging together with Scripture and the teachings of the Church. It is a two-way process that will help others understand us better too.

Listening also helps us to pay attention to the **POWER** in relationships. Philippians 2 describes how, in Jesus, God 'emptied himself', choosing to humble himself, rather than exploiting the divine power that he could have used. Many factors can lead to an imbalance of power – for example age, gender, ethnicity, education and economic status.

Power is particularly noticeable when the decisions of others impact our lives. They may be decisions about our work, family or home, for example. Sometimes people have powerful personalities that make it difficult for us to challenge them. When people are aware of their power and don't misuse it, there can be good and healthy relationships. An abuse of power, however, especially over people who are marginalized or vulnerable, can be devastating.

In church communities, ordained and lay church leaders often have power through their role, their knowledge or the control they have over buildings or money. It is important to be aware of these power dynamics especially in discussions about difference. The challenge for anyone in church leadership is Jesus' subversive call to servant leadership: '... whoever wishes to become great among you must be your servant' (Mark 10.43).

Here are some questions for you to discuss as a group.

Think about situations when you found it hard to listen to someone, or particular people you find it hard to listen well to. Share these with each other: why was it hard to listen?

Think about a time when you've struggled – or failed – to speak up, perhaps within your church community.

- What was going on?
- How was power manifested in the relationship?

Think about a time when you were spoken to in an unhelpful way, even if it was intended to be helpful.

- What made it unhelpful?
- What did you do?
- What could you have done?

How is power used in your church, visibly and invisibly (both well and not so well)?

In what ways might your church community become more aware of the use of power and take greater care in this regard?

④ Homework

Notice the conversations you have in any particular day.

At the end of the day, choose one conversation:

- Replay it in your mind and think about how you listened and spoke.
- What, on reflection, might you have done differently?
- How was your understanding deepened?

⑤ Act of Worship

Finish the session with the short Act of Worship found on page 32.

SESSION ②

Talking about confidence and casting out **FEAR**

The AIMS of this session are

- To become aware of our fears, both as individuals and as members of our church community

- To reflect on how we can help to create relationships and a community that helps people to feel safe

SESSION 2

1 Course film

Watch the Session 2 video.

2 Bible study

John 7.53—8.11

Then each of them went home, [1]while Jesus went to the Mount of Olives. [2]Early in the morning he came again to the temple. All the people came to him and he sat down and began to teach them. [3]The scribes and the Pharisees brought a woman who had been caught in adultery; and making her stand before all of them, [4]they said to him, 'Teacher, this woman was caught in the very act of committing adultery. [5]Now in the law Moses commanded us to stone such women. Now what do you say?' [6]They said this to test him, so that they might have some charge to bring against him. Jesus bent down and wrote with his finger on the ground. [7]When they kept on questioning him, he straightened up and said to them, 'Let anyone among you who is without sin be the first to throw a stone at her.' [8]And once again he bent down and wrote on the ground. [9]When they heard it, they went away, one by one, beginning with the elders; and Jesus was left alone with the woman standing before him. [10]Jesus straightened up and said to her, 'Woman, where are they? Has no one condemned you?' [11]She said, 'No one, sir.' And Jesus said, 'Neither do I condemn you. Go your way, and from now on do not sin again.'

Here are some questions for you to discuss as a group.

- Who is afraid in this story and why?
- Whose fears do you identify with in the story?
- What does this story say about addressing the problem of fear in our churches?

③ Reflect and discuss together

Learning together in a group can be an enriching and stimulating experience. But it can also be scary. We may be fearful of some of the people in the group, and we may be fearful about being asked to explore perspectives with which we disagree and which affect our lives.

FEAR can cause us to feel unable to speak out, or to be who we are. We may fear someone else's reaction to what we say. We may be worried that others will think less of us or cause us to feel shame even when there is no reason for it. We may fear that we will no longer truly belong to the church community in which we worship, seek fellowship, or minister. As a result we may move further to the margins or even leave. It is a terrible thing to feel fear in the Church, which should be a space of acceptance and safety.

We all experience fear in our lives and we all have the capacity to make others feel fearful. The Bible tells us that perfect love casts out fear (1 John 4.18). So we need to help each other to be careful, sensitive and compassionate in all our relationships, remembering how easily we can hurt and be hurt. We also need to be on the lookout for people who are on the margins of our church communities – or even absent – because of fear. It is often those who have little voice who need to be given confidence to speak out. How can we give those people space?

Here is an activity for you to do as a group.

Take a moment to become aware of situations in which you find yourself fearful and name them to yourself.

The group leader hands out pieces of paper and pens to each person. Write one fear on each piece of paper – using as many as you'd like. Don't write your name on the paper.

When everyone has had an opportunity to do this, pass a basket or bowl around and ask people to put the pieces of paper in the bowl.*

The leader then takes them out, one by one, and reads what is on them, in silence and prayer.

Encourage the members of the group to 'own' or reflect on these fears, thinking especially how they might play out in their own church context.

Think about 1 John 4.18 and how we can help each other to be more free of fear.

If you are doing this in an online meeting, then you can use free software like 'Google jamboard' (using 'post-its'), a Zoom whiteboard or a 'Mentimeter word cloud' to do this exercise.

4 Homework

Think ahead to some of the encounters you will have over the coming week.

- Is there one you are nervous about?
- What might you do to change that dynamic?

After the encounter, reflect on what happened, what you learned and what you might do differently next time.

5 Act of Worship

Finish the session with the short Act of Worship found on page 32.

Talking about respect and acknowledging **PREJUDICE**

The AIMS of this session are

- To become aware of some of our prejudices as individuals and as a church community

- To explore how we can help each other to address some of the prejudices that affect our relationships and attitudes

① Course film

Watch the Session 3 video.

② Bible study

John 4.5–30, 39–42

⁵So he came to a Samaritan city called Sychar, near the plot of ground that Jacob had given to his son Joseph. ⁶Jacob's well was there, and Jesus, tired out by his journey, was sitting by the well. It was about noon.

⁷ A Samaritan woman came to draw water, and Jesus said to her, 'Give me a drink'. ⁸(His disciples had gone to the city to buy food.) ⁹The Samaritan woman said to him, 'How is it that you, a Jew, ask a drink of me, a woman of Samaria?' (Jews do not share things in common with Samaritans.) ¹⁰Jesus answered her, 'If you knew the gift of God, and who it is that is saying to you, "Give me a drink", you would have asked him, and he would have given you living water.' ¹¹The woman said to him, 'Sir, you have no bucket, and the well is deep. Where do you get that living water? ¹²Are you greater than our ancestor Jacob, who gave us the well, and with his sons and his flocks drank from it?' ¹³Jesus said to her, 'Everyone who drinks of this water will be thirsty again, ¹⁴but those who drink of the water that I will give them will never be thirsty. The water that I will give will become in them a spring of water gushing up to eternal life.' ¹⁵The woman said to him, 'Sir, give me this water, so that I may never be thirsty or have to keep coming here to draw water.'

¹⁶ Jesus said to her, 'Go, call your husband, and come back.' ¹⁷The woman answered him, 'I have no husband.' Jesus said to her, 'You are right in saying, "I have no husband"; ¹⁸for you have had five husbands, and the one you have now is not your husband.

What you have said is true!' ¹⁹The woman said to him, 'Sir, I see that you are a prophet. ²⁰Our ancestors worshipped on this mountain, but you say that the place where people must worship is in Jerusalem.' ²¹Jesus said to her, 'Woman, believe me, the hour is coming when you will worship the Father neither on this mountain nor in Jerusalem. ²²You worship what you do not know; we worship what we know, for salvation is from the Jews. ²³But the hour is coming, and is now here, when the true worshippers will worship the Father in spirit and truth, for the Father seeks such as these to worship him. ²⁴God is spirit, and those who worship him must worship in spirit and truth.' ²⁵The woman said to him, 'I know that Messiah is coming' (who is called Christ). 'When he comes, he will proclaim all things to us.' ²⁶Jesus said to her, 'I am he, the one who is speaking to you.'

²⁷ Just then his disciples came. They were astonished that he was speaking with a woman, but no one said, 'What do you want?' or, 'Why are you speaking with her?' ²⁸Then the woman left her water-jar and went back to the city. She said to the people, ²⁹'Come and see a man who told me everything I have ever done! He cannot be the Messiah, can he?' ³⁰They left the city and were on their way to him. [...]

³⁹ Many Samaritans from that city believed in him because of the woman's testimony, 'He told me everything I have ever done.' ⁴⁰So when the Samaritans came to him, they asked him to stay with them; and he stayed there for two days. ⁴¹And many more believed because of his word. ⁴²They said to the woman, 'It is no longer because of what you said that we believe, for we have heard for ourselves, and we know that this is truly the Saviour of the world.'

Here are some questions for you to discuss as a group.

- What prejudices are at work here?
- How does the woman respond to prejudice? What about the disciples? And Jesus himself?
- What might it mean for the church to mirror Jesus' response to the woman?

③ Reflect and discuss together

As individuals we are all prejudiced in one way or another. What's more, we tend to be blind to our own prejudices and quick to see those of others. Often without even realizing it, it is our prejudices that shape our decisions and allegiances, rather than our desire to seek the truth. Prejudices may relate to many aspects of our lives: religion, ethnicity and race, gender, age, politics, social or relational status, are just some examples. Helping each other to become more aware of how prejudices affect our relationships and witness to Christ is a challenging task.

PREJUDICE is one of the ways in which a group of people can create an identity. Identifying with and being loyal to a particular group over and against those outside it can foster prejudice. Sometimes called 'tribalism', this kind of power and control to create group cohesion has blighted society throughout history. And it happens in the Church too. We separate ourselves from each other by the way we 'do' or 'don't do' church. We decide who is 'in' and who is 'out' for whatever reason. These attitudes and behaviours weaken the Church. At a time when the Church is coming to terms with its changing place in society, and with fewer resources to share, the temptation to retreat into factions and echo chambers is great.

Jesus calls us to 'love your neighbour as yourself' (Matthew 22.37–39). Becoming more aware of our prejudices will help us to love people who are different from us, whether they are our neighbours on our street or in our church communities.

Here are some questions for you to discuss as a group.

Name some of prejudices prevalent in our society.

- What are some stereotypes that prejudices give rise to?
- How have you experienced prejudice or being stereotyped?

Reflect together about the prejudices you, as individuals, might have and how they affect your behaviour and attitudes.

What about your church community? Might there be people who would experience prejudice in your life together?

How can we be more active in helping each other to recognize, acknowledge and overcome prejudice?

 Homework

Next time you are out and about, notice the people around you on the street or in the shop, and listen to the unspoken judgments you might be making about them. Or when watching TV/listening to the radio: what do you notice about your unspoken judgements about people. What stereotypes do you see portrayed on TV and in films? Pray for each individual you notice, remembering the depth of God's love for them.

5 Act of Worship

Finish the session with the short Act of Worship found on page 32.

Talking about openness and speaking into **SILENCE**

The AIMS of this session are

- To pay attention to the areas of life about which we as individuals and as a church community are silent

- To reflect on the impact of silence on our relationships and life as a church

- To learn about ways to address unhelpful silence in our church community

① Course film

Watch the Session 4 video.

② Bible study

Luke 8.43–48

[43] Now there was a woman who had been suffering from haemorrhages for twelve years; and though she had spent all she had on physicians, no one could cure her. [44]She came up behind him and touched the fringe of his clothes, and immediately her haemorrhage stopped. [45]Then Jesus asked, 'Who touched me?' When all denied it, Peter said, 'Master, the crowds surround you and press in on you.' [46]But Jesus said, 'Someone touched me; for I noticed that power had gone out from me.' [47]When the woman saw that she could not remain hidden, she came trembling; and falling down before him, she declared in the presence of all the people why she had touched him, and how she had been immediately healed. [48]He said to her, 'Daughter, your faith has made you well; go in peace.'

Here are some questions for you to discuss as a group.

Jesus compels the woman from being silent about her condition to having to tell her story in public.

- Why did the woman want to remain hidden?

- What was the reward for her openness?

- Read on to the end of the chapter in your Bible/online. Thinking about verse 49, what might prevent you from taking the time to encourage people who are reluctant to speak from doing so?

③ Reflect and discuss together

Within the Christian traditions, silence is usually associated with the contemplative life of prayer. As a spiritual discipline, silence can help us become more aware of God's presence and more able to hear God's voice. Silence is a good thing to develop as part of our prayers and worship. It is helpful for our discipleship.

SILENCE can also be very destructive. A culture of silence within a church community can be used to shelter abuses of power. Distressingly, this has been illustrated very clearly by the recent independent inquiry into sexual abuse within the Church. Some people in authority had not acted as they should have done to protect children and young people, and others had not spoken out on behalf of victims because of feelings of deference or fear.

A culture of silence within a church community can also be used to avoid controversy. It is often said that, 'We don't talk about religion and politics.' We could add sexuality and money to this, too, and probably more. These are seen as private and divisive matters to be avoided. The problem is that we now don't know how to talk about these things, and this is not serving us well. Silence has fostered a culture around these issues which is marked by a lack of knowledge and understanding, and has created a vacuum which is being filled by prejudice, fear, and misinformation. Our reluctance to talk with each other about these matters with respect and openness hinders our ability to learn, and to welcome people who are different to us. It hinders our discipleship.

Here are some questions for you to discuss as a group.

Think back to your family when you were growing up.

- Were there subjects that you never talked about?

Now think about your church family.

- What areas of life are rarely spoken about?

You might want to repeat the activity you did in Session 2, writing the things you think the Church is silent about on the pieces of paper.

- What are some of the reasons you have been silent or have known others to be silent in church when it would have been better to speak?
- What can we do to enable ourselves and others to speak in such situations?

4 Homework

Fears and prejudices can feed a culture of oppressive silence. One way of overcoming these is by getting to know each other better. Consider how you might befriend someone in your church or small group who you don't know very well.

5 Act of Worship

Finish the session with the short Act of Worship found on page 32.

SESSION ⑤

Talking about integrity and admitting **HYPOCRISY**

The AIMS of this session are

- To examine and confess some of the ways in which we, as individuals and as a church community, may be guilty of hypocrisy – of saying one thing and doing another

- To find ways of encouraging each other to be both honest and humble in our words and behaviours

---

① Course film

Watch the Session 5 video.

② Bible study

Matthew 7.1–5

'Do not judge, so that you may not be judged. [2]For with the judgement you make you will be judged, and the measure you give will be the measure you get. [3]Why do you see the speck in your neighbour's eye, but do not notice the log in your own eye? [4]Or how can you say to your neighbour, "Let me take the speck out of your eye", while the log is in your own eye? [5]You hypocrite, first take the log out of your own eye, and then you will see clearly to take the speck out of your neighbour's eye.'

Matthew 23.23–26

'Woe to you, scribes and Pharisees, hypocrites! For you tithe mint, dill, and cummin, and have neglected the weightier matters of the law: justice and mercy and faith. It is these you ought to have practised without neglecting the others. [24]You blind guides! You strain out a gnat but swallow a camel!

[25] 'Woe to you, scribes and Pharisees, hypocrites! For you clean the outside of the cup and of the plate, but inside they are full of greed and self-indulgence. [26]You blind Pharisee! First clean the inside of the cup, so that the outside also may become clean.'

Here are some questions for you to discuss as a group.

Judgmentalism, a disregard for true justice and a preoccupation with appearances are all condemned under the banner of hypocrisy.

- How are these kinds of behaviours seen in us?
- How and when do we see them in our churches?

③ Reflect and discuss together

If we ask people what they see in the church, the answer will often sadly include, '**HYPOCRISY**'. They hear the good news of Jesus Christ, but do not see it being lived out in the lives of his followers. They feel judged by the church about their lives, and their lifestyles, but they see the same issues in the people of God, poking through a veneer of religious respectability.

None of us live the perfect life, and all of us have issues that we grapple with. Even St Paul acknowledged this about his own life: 'I can will what is right, but I cannot do it. For I do not do the good I want, but the evil I do not want is what I do' (Romans 7.18b–19). We are a work in progress, as we grow in our discipleship. In Jesus Christ, God has shown us a way for living. God, knowing our frailty and fallibility, also shows us profound grace, and mercy, as we seek to follow Christ. We are called to show the same grace and mercy to others.

In a world of misinformation, with public institutions and leaders trusted less than they used to be, people are yearning for authenticity and integrity. They want a place to be fully themselves, with people who are genuine and open about who they are.

They don't need Christians to be perfect, but they do need us to be honest about our lives and walk with God, so that they can find this same hope for themselves, and feel that they too can be part of the Body of Christ without feeling fear or shame.

Here are some questions for you to discuss as a group.

It's not easy to see our own hypocrisy and it's even harder to admit it.

* How can each of us help our own church community to be more honest and humble?
* Are there areas in the wider Church of inconsistency or hypocrisy that you think need to be admitted and confessed?

4 Homework

This is the last session of the Course. If you haven't already adopted this habit, consider using a form of daily 'examen' at the end of each day:

* As you become aware of God's presence, replay the events of the day, and your thoughts and feelings about them.
* Recall moments for which to give God thanks and praise.
* Recall moments which prompt you to confess and repent: when you didn't pay attention to power, address ignorance, cast out fear, acknowledge prejudice, speak into silence or admit hypocrisy.
* As a forgiven and beloved child of God, rest in God's promise of a new day and a fresh start tomorrow.

5 Act of Worship

Finish the session with the short Act of Worship found on page 32.

A SIMPLE ACT OF WORSHIP

to end each session

Everyone says all of the words in bold print together, and someone is chosen to read the Bible passage.

In the name of the Father, and of the Son, and of the Holy Spirit. Amen.

Bible reading

Read the passage from the Bible study at the start of the session.

Holy God, you have heard our discussion, and you know our thoughts.
Open our eyes, that we might see you in the stranger.
Open our hearts, that we might share your love with others.

Blessed are the poor in spirit, for theirs is the kingdom of heaven.
Blessed are those who mourn, for they will be comforted.
Blessed are the meek, for they will inherit the earth.
Blessed are those who hunger and thirst for righteousness,
**   for they will be filled.**
Blessed are the merciful, for they will receive mercy.
Blessed are the pure in heart, for they will see God.
Blessed are the peacemakers, for they will be called children of God.
Blessed are those who are persecuted for righteousness' sake,
**   for theirs is the kingdom of heaven.**

Matthew 5.2–10